SHORELINES

Sally Morgan & Pauline Lalor

SIMON & SCHUSTER
YOUNG BOOKS

Our planet has many different environments in which a rich variety of plants and animals make their homes. These environments are unique, but they are all under threat — from the growing human population, its industry and its pollution. Young readers can't protect fragile environments unless they understand them. The Living World gives insight into these special areas and makes positive suggestions for their future management.

Commissioning editor: Daphne Butler
Book editor: Claire Llewellyn
Design and artwork: SPL Design
Photographs: Ecoscene, except for
RSPB (6, 21t)
Zefa (12l)
Nature Photographers Ltd (21bl)
Typesetting and layout: Quark Xpress

First published in Great Britain in 1992
by Simon & Schuster Young Books

Simon & Schuster Young Books
Campus 400, Maylands Avenue
Hemel Hempstead, Herts HP2 7EZ

Printed and bound in Portugal
by Edições ASA

A catalogue record for this book
is available from the British Library
ISBN 0 7500 1098 3

(Opposite title page)
The sea is so powerful it washes up the trunks of huge redwood trees—Washington State, USA.

Contents

Where the sea meets the land	6-7
Waves and tides	8-9
Cliffs	10-11
Rocky shores	12-13
Rockpools	14-15
Sandy beaches	16-17
Sand dunes	18-19
Estuaries	20-21
Mangrove swamps	22-23
People on the shoreline	24-25
Polluted shores	26-27
Planning for the future	28-29
Index	30

6 Where the sea meets the land

All around the world

Much of our planet is covered with water — almost three-quarters of its surface. Where the sea meets the land, the world's shorelines stretch for thousands of kilometres around every island and continent. There are sandy beaches, sticky mudflats, oozing swamps and dramatic rocky shorelines.

Homes for wildlife

Shorelines are particularly interesting because they are not very wide and yet they are the meeting place between land and sea. A rich variety of plants and animals make their homes there.

A changing environment

Shorelines are never the same for very long. Sometimes the land is exposed, while at other times it is covered by deep, salt water. The pounding of the waves churns up the sand and breaks the rocks.

The animals and plants that live on the shore have all adapted in some way to survive in such a changing environment.

Shorelines stretch for thousands of kilometres. These cliffs meet the sea on the Pacific coast, California, USA. ►

◄ *On the shore, animals must adapt to an ever-changing environment . Here, Brent geese search for food in the mud as soon as the tide falls.*

7

Waves and tides

Wind and waves

Waves wash shorelines every minute of every day and night. Sometimes they are gentle ripples but in storms they crash onto the land with great force. They are caused by the wind blowing across the wide stretches of water far out at sea.

The tides

Twice a day the sea rises up the shore and then goes back again. High tide is when the sea comes up the shore. Low tide is when it has moved back down and the beach is exposed. In some places the difference between high and low tides is very great but in others it may be less than a metre.

Plants and animals that live between the high and low tide marks have a difficult life. Twice a day, when the tide is out, they are exposed to predators and to the drying effects of sun and wind. Six hours later, when the tide is in, they are submerged beneath salt water.

A river runs into the sea in a bay in Wales. The pictures opposite show the same scene six hours apart. What differences can you see? ➢

➢ *Have you ever felt the power of waves as they pound onto the beach?*

Cliffs

▲ *Steep cliffs, like these on the south coast of England, have narrow ledges where plants or birds may perch. What type of rock are the cliffs?*

At the edge of the land

Some shores have high cliffs which tower above the water. They were formed millions of years ago when the land was pushed up, leaving a high edge next to the sea. As the waves crash against the bottom of the cliff, its edge crumbles away and falls into the sea. This is called erosion.

Living on the edge

Cliffs are often very windy places, and in winter they can be very cold indeed. The air is salty, filled with tiny drops of water blown up from the sea. Salt is harsh and dries things out. These conditions make life difficult for the plants and animals that live here.

Plants need long roots to hold them firmly in the cracks in the cliffs. Not much rain reaches them on the cliff face, so many of the plants have thick, fleshy leaves in which they store water. Plants which grow on the cliff top are very low, and cling to the ground to keep out of the wind.

Safe for birds

Colonies of sea birds nest on the narrow ledges of the cliffs. Here, they can lay their eggs safely away from predators. These colonies are very noisy places with birds shrieking to each other above the sound of the wind and sea. There is also a strong smell of fish. Can you think why?

▲ *A kittiwake nests on a narrow ledge on a cliff face.*

Pink thrift is a low-growing plant that thrives on windy cliff tops. ▼

Rocky shores

How are they made?

Many shores are covered in rocks which have broken off from the cliffs. Some rocks are very hard but others, such as white chalk and limestone, are softer. Sometimes, when these rocks split open, you can find fossils inside. These are the remains of plants and animals which died thousands of years ago. They were covered by mud and turned into stone.

As incoming tides stream over rocks, they gradually change and erode them. ►

Turned into stone — this spade fish lived 50 million years ago. ▼

The three kinds of seaweed in this picture vary according to their shape and colour. Can you see them? ►

Seaweeds

Many rocky beaches are covered with seaweed. Seaweeds are plants, but they don't have roots like a plant in the garden. Instead, they have a root-like end, called a holdfast, which grips the rock. Seaweeds use sunlight to make their food, like plants on land. They can survive a long time out of water, so are well suited to life on the shore.

Home on the rocks

Many plants and animals live among the rocks. The ones that live near the top of the shore have adapted to being out of water for long periods of time. Limpets are animals which clamp themselves tightly to a rock to avoid losing any water. Others, like sea anemones, live lower down the shore where they are covered by water most of the time. They die if they dry out.

Limpets and tiny barnacles cling to rocks, and are almost impossible to remove. ▼

Rockpools

How do rockpools form?

When the tide goes out, seawater is left behind in the dips and hollows of the rocks. These little pools are cut off from the sea until the tide rises again. This may be for just an hour or two, or it may be for many days.

Many plants and animals live in the pools caught between the rocks when the tide goes out.▼

Miniature worlds

Under the water, seaweeds are attached firmly to the rocks. Small fish and snails hide among their fronds. Crabs hide too — under stones at the bottom of the pool. They wait for small animals to pass by and then catch them using their large claws. Limpets, protected by their hard shells, cling to the rocks.

▲ *Dog whelks, mussels and tiny barnacles cling to the rocks. The brightly coloured dog whelks feed on the mussels.*

Sea anemones look like flowers, but they are really predators. They catch smaller animals, like tiny fish, with their sticky tentacles. ▼

Food chains

Crabs eat snails, snails eat seaweeds. This is called a food chain. Can you think of any other food chains — not by the sea, but in your own garden, for example?

▲ *You may find starfish in a rockpool. They eat mussels by forcing the closed shell open with surprising strength. They have five arms and a very rough spiny skin. If one arm is damaged or breaks off, the starfish grows a new one.*

Sandy beaches

What is sand?

It is hard to believe that sand is the result of erosion. For thousands of years, powerful waves have pounded against cliffs and broken them into rocks. In turn, the rocks have been pounded into tiny grains of sand. The sea carries the sand along the coast, and washes it up on the shore where it forms a beach. The shells of sea animals also get broken up and added to the sand.

Sand is always on the move as waves wash over its surface. No seaweeds grow here — they cannot settle in the moving sand.

The strand line

Near the top of the beach is the strand line — a tangled line of seaweed, dead animals and rubbish, washed up by the tide. Birds scavenge here, along with tiny sandhoppers that come out at night.

◄ *There is no sign of life on this deserted sandy beach in the Seychelles.*

Hiding in the sand

Sandy beaches often look deserted, but hidden beneath the sand are hundreds of animals. When the tide is out they burrow into the sand to hide from the sun, wind and predators. As the tide rises and covers the beach, these animals come out of hiding to feed on food carried in by the tide.

A ghost crab burrows into a sandy beach on the Indian Ocean. ▼

Sand dunes

Blown by the wind

Along some beaches the sea washes up more sand with every tide. When the wind blows off the sea onto the land, it blows the dry sand behind the beach into small hills of sand which we call dunes.

The roots of marram grass stop the sand from blowing away and help dunes to form in Dorset, England. ▼

Living on shifting sand

Dry sand, which is always moving in the wind, is a difficult place for plants to grow. A few are able to grow on the dunes, and their roots help to stop the sand from blowing away. This makes it easier for other plants to grow, so that after a long period of time the dune will be covered by many different plants.

▲ *Sandwich terns nest in the shelter of the dunes.*

Rabbits make a warm, dry home for themselves behind the dunes. ▼

A sheltered habitat

Many birds make their nests in sand dunes because they are sheltered and the sand is warm. Rabbits often burrow in the soft, sandy ground behind the dunes. They dig many tunnels which link together to form a warren.

Estuaries

▲ *Huge expanses of mud are exposed at low tide in Cardiff Bay, Wales.*

How are estuaries formed?

An estuary is the place where a large river flows into the sea, mixing its fresh water with the salty water of the sea.

As a river flows downstream, tiny bits of sand and mud are swept along in the water. When it reaches the estuary, the river moves much more slowly, which makes all the sand and mud sink to the river bed. Over many years a muddy layer builds up, forming mudflats. These are covered by water at high tide but, when the tide goes out, the mud is exposed to the air.

A rich larder

Many people think that estuaries are muddy wastelands. They couldn't be more wrong. The mud may be smelly and gooey, but it contains a huge number of living creatures. One bucketful of mud will be teeming with worms, snails and prawns. As a result, great flocks of birds come to estuaries to feed at low tide.

▲ *The long, pointed beak of the dunlin probes for food in the mud.*

Special beaks

The shape of a bird's beak tells you a lot about the way it feeds. Some birds have spoon-like beaks to scoop up small fish. Others have up-turned beaks which are good for sieving mud. Long, pointed beaks provide a sharp tool for digging. Can you think of any other kinds of beak?

The spoonbill has a long, spoon-shaped beak which is ideal for scooping up small fish. ►

The avocet uses its curved beak to sweep seawater for shrimps and small fish. ▼

Mangrove swamps

What are mangrove swamps?

In the hottest parts of the world, near the equator, some estuaries form mangrove swamps instead of mudflats.

These swamps are eerie places. The air is hot and sticky, and the smell of mud is overpowering. There are strange noises — dripping water from the trees, the odd clicks and plops made by snails and crabs, and the steady whine of mosquitoes.

Remarkable trees

Only a special type of tree called a mangrove can grow in the thick mud. Mangroves are odd trees which can look as if they are on stilts. The stilts are really roots which grow down into the water and mud to support the tree. The tangled roots make an ideal place for young fish to grow up before swimming out to sea.

There is so little oxygen in mud that the mangrove sends up short aerial roots to take in air.

A battalion of soldier crabs comes out to feed on the muddy swamp in Queensland, Australia.

Food in the mud

There is a lot of food in the mud — fallen leaves, tiny plants and dead animals. At low tide a huge army of small animals comes out to feed on this feast. Then, larger predators like monkeys, snakes and birds move in to prey on the smaller animals.

People on the shoreline

Too many visitors

During this century, shorelines have become very popular places. Most people enjoy playing on the beach and swimming in the sea.

Unfortunately, as soon as people crowd a place, they begin to spoil it. They leave litter, destroy habitats and scare away animals.

▲ *Rubbish on a beach in Dorset, southern England.*

Beautiful coastlines have been spoilt by tourism, as here in Mallorca, Spain. ▼

▲ *Where is the shoreline? This coast in Gibraltar has been transformed by a marina, an airstrip and development.*

Building destroys habitats

Huge resorts are built beside long, sandy beaches. In the tropics, mangrove swamps are cleared to make way for hotels. Changes like this destroy the natural habitats of plants and animals.

In sheltered estuaries glittering marinas are replacing the quiet mudflats. Estuaries are also chosen as sites for oil refineries and ports because ships can reach them by sea or river. This kind of development makes thousands of birds homeless, and many eventually die.

Polluted shores

▲ *All washed up — a dead seabird, covered with oil.*

Oil kills

Every day, shorelines are being damaged by pollution. Some kinds of pollution are hard to see — but not oil. Huge amounts of oil are transported around the world daily in large ships called tankers. If a tanker has an accident, its cargo may spill into the sea. Oil floats on water, sometimes forming a slick several kilometres wide. Eventually, it is washed up on the coast and covers the shoreline, and its wildlife, with a black, sticky film.

◀ *Thick foam from chemical pollution covers this rocky shore in Wales.*

Poisoning the sea

For too long the sea has been used as a dumping ground for waste which cannot be easily disposed of on land. Sewage — human waste from toilets — is pumped out to sea in pipes. It can be treated to make it safe and clean, but sometimes raw, untreated sewage is put into the sea. The germs it contains make the water unsafe for swimming, and unsafe for the plants and animals which live there.

Planning the future

Nature reserves

One way to preserve some of our shorelines is to turn them into nature reserves. Plants and animals inside reserves are protected. People may only visit certain areas of the reserve, perhaps only at certain times, and they may need a special pass to do so. Building of any kind is not allowed.

In Britain, the National Trust is buying as much of the shoreline as possible in order to protect it from pollution and development.

Cleaning the water

Stricter laws would help to stop the dumping of sewage and other waste in the sea. In Europe, there is now a scheme which awards a blue flag to beaches which are clean and safe.

A beach near Poole, England flies the European blue flag to show the beach is clean and safe. ►

Dunk Island, on the Great Barrier Reef off Australia, is a unique environment and forms part of a nature reserve. ▼

1990
ALL
DONATIONS
GRATEFULLY
RECEIVED

Index

birds 6, 11, 17, 19, 20, 23, 25, 27
building 25, 28

cliff 6, 10, 12, 17
crabs 14, 17, 23

erosion 10, 12, 17, 30
estuary 20, 23, 25

fish 11, 14, 15, 21, 23
fossil 12

mangrove 23, 25
mudflat 6, 20, 23

nature reserve 28

oil 25, 27

plants 6, 8, 10, 11, 12, 13, 14, 18, 23, 27, 28
pollution 26, 27, 28
predators 8, 11, 15, 17, 23

river 8, 20, 25
rockpool 14, 15
rocks 6, 10, 12, 14, 17, 30

salt 6, 8, 10, 20
sand 6, 17, 18, 19, 20, 25
sand dune 18, 19
seaweed 13, 14, 15, 17
sewage 27, 28
swamp 6, 22, 23, 25

tide 8, 12, 14, 17, 18, 20, 23

waves 6, 8, 10, 17, 30
wind 8, 10, 11, 17, 18

The power of the sea: waves eroded this huge rock pinnacle on a beach in Washington State, USA. ►